THE PEARL

SOPHIE JEWETT

Copyright © 2015 Sophie Jewett

All rights reserved.

ISBN: 1515298485
ISBN-13: 978-1515298489

THE PEARL

To KATHARINE LEE BATES

THE TRANSLATOR TO THE AUTHOR

Poet of beauty, pardon me
If touch of mine have tarnishèd
Thy Pearl's pure luster, loved by thee;
Or dimmed thy vision of the dead
Alive in light and gaiety.
Thy life is like a shadow fled;
Thy place we know not nor degree,
The stock that bore thee, school that bred;
Yet shall thy fame be sung and said.
Poet of wonder, pain, and peace,
Hold high thy nameless, laurelled head
Where Dante dwells with Beatrice.

PREFACE

Among the treasures of the British Museum is a manuscript which contains four anonymous poems, apparently of common authorship: "The Pearl," "Cleanness," "Patience," "Sir Gawayne and the Green Knight." From the language of the writer, it seems clear that he was a native of some Northwestern district of England, and that he lived in the second half of the Fourteenth Century. He is quite unknown, save as his work reveals him, a man of aristocratic breeding, of religious and secular education, of a deeply emotional and spiritual nature, gifted with imagination and perception of beauty. He shows a liking for technique that leads him to adopt elaborate devices of rhyme, while retaining the alliteration characteristic of Northern Middle English verse. He wrote as was the fashion of his time, allegory, homily, lament, chivalric romance, but the distinction of his poetry is that of a finely accentuated individuality.

The poems called "Cleanness" and "Patience," retell incidents of biblical history for a definitely didactic purpose, but even these are frequently lifted into the region of imaginative literature by the author's power of graphic description. "Sir Gawayne and the Green Knight" is a priceless contribution to Arthurian story. "The Pearl," though it takes the form of symbolic narrative, is essentially lyric and elegiac, the lament, it would seem, of a father for a little, long-lost daughter.

The present translation of "The Pearl" was begun with no larger design than that of turning a few passages into modern English, by way of illustrating to a group of students engaged in reading the original, the possibility of preserving intricate stanzaic form, and something of alliteration, without an entire sacrifice of poetic beauty. The experiment was persisted in because its problems are such as baffle and fascinate a translator, and the finished version is offered not merely to students of Middle English but to college classes in the history of English literature, and to non-academic readers.

If "The Pearl" presented no greater obstacle to a modern reader than is offered by Chaucer's English, a translation might be a gratuitous task, but the Northwest-Midland dialect of the poem is, in fact, incomparably more difficult than the diction of Chaucer, more difficult even than that of Langland. The meaning of many passages remains obscure, and a translator is often forced to choose what seems the least dubious among doubtful readings.

The poem in the original passes frequently from imaginative beauty to conversational commonplace, from deep feeling to didactic aphorism or theological dogma, and it has been my endeavor faithfully to interpret these variations of matter and of style, sometimes substituting modern colloquialisms for such as are obsolete, or in other ways paraphrasing a stubborn passage, but striving never to polish the dullest lines nor to strengthen the weakest.

A reader who will observe the difficult rhyming scheme, a scheme that calls for six words of one rhyme and four of another, will understand the presence of forced lines, an intrusion that one must needs suffer in even "The Faerie Queene." These padded lines are a serious blemish to the poem, but the introduction of naïve and familiar expressions is one of its charms, as when the Pearl, protesting like Piccarda in Paradise[1] that among beatified spirits there can be no rivalry, exclaims: "The more the merrier."

The translation may, at many points, need apology, but the original needs only explanation. Readers familiar with mediæval poetry expect to encounter moral platitudes and theological subtlety. Dogma takes large and vital place in the sublimest cantos of Dante's "Paradise," and the English poet is consciously following his noblest master when he puts a sermon into the lips of his "little queen." To modern ears such exposition is at harsh discord with the simple human grief and longing of the poet, but to the mediaevalist symbolic theology was a passion. Precisely in the moment when she begins a discourse concerning the doctrine of redemption, Beatrice turns upon Dante "eyes that might make a man happy in the fire," and at its close he looks upon her and beholds her "grow more beautiful." If even Beatrice has been considered mere personification, it is natural that the Pearl should be so regarded, but the plain reader finds in the symbolic maiden of the English poem, as in the transfigured lady of the Italian, some record of a human being whose loss was anguish, and whose presence rapture, to a poet long ago.

The lover of things mediæval will find in this little book not only the familiar garden of Guillaume de Lorris, of Boccaccio and of Chaucer, but an unexpected and enchanting vision of great forest and rushing water, of hillside and plain, of crystal cliffs and flame-winged birds; of the Pearl among her white peers; of the Apocalyptic Jerusalem, discovered to the poet, it may be, as a goodly Gothic city, though its walls are built of precious stone, and its towers rise from neither church nor minster.

If even a few readers turn from the modern to the original version, the translation will have had fair fortune, for the author of "The Pearl" is, though unknown and unnamed, a poet second only to Chaucer in Chaucer's generation.

It is a pleasure to record my many debts of gratitude: to Professor Frank H. Chase of Beloit, Professor John L. Lowes of Swarthmore, and Dr. Charles G. Osgood of Princeton, for their careful reading of the translation in manuscript, with invaluable assistance and suggestion; to Professor Martha Hale Shackford, and Miss Laura A. Hibbard, for constant aid while the work was in making, and, above all, to Professor Katharine Lee Bates for a critical, line by line, comparison of this version with the original.

[Footnote 1: Par. III.]

[Footnote 2: Pearl, stanza 71.]

[Footnote 3: Par. VII, II. 17-18; Par. VIII, I. 15.]

S.J.
WELLESLEY COLLEGE,
June, 1908.

EDITIONS: R. Morris, Early English text Sc. 1864; I. Gollancz, London, 1891; C.G. Osgood, Boston, 1906 (with admirable introduction, etc.). TRANSLATIONS: Gollancz (above); S. Weir Mitchell, New York, 1906 (poetic, but incomplete); G.G. Coulton, London, 1906 (metre of the original); C.G. Osgood, Princeton, 1907 (prose).

THE PEARL

I

Pearl that the Prince full well might prize,
So surely set in shining gold!
No pearl of Orient with her vies;
To prove her peerless I make bold:
So round, so radiant to mine eyes,
smooth she seemed, so small to hold,
Among all jewels judges wise
Would count her best an hundred fold.
Alas! I lost my pearl of old!
I pine with heart-pain unforgot;
Down through my arbour grass it rolled,
My own pearl, precious, without spot.

Since in that spot it slipped from me
I wait, and wish, and oft complain;
Once it would bid my sorrow flee,
And my fair fortune turn again;
It wounds my heart now ceaselessly,
And burns my breast with bitter pain.
Yet never so sweet a song may be
As, this still hour, steals through my brain,
While verity I muse in vain
How clay should her bright beauty clot;
O Earth! a brave gem thou dost stain,
My own pearl, precious, without spot!

Needs must that spot with spices spread,
Where such wealth falleth to decay;
Fair flowers, golden and blue and red,
Shine in the sunlight day by day;

Nor flower nor fruit have witherèd
On turf wherein such treasure lay;
The blade grows where the grain lies dead,
Else were no ripe wheat stored away;
Of good come good things, so we say,
Then surely such seed faileth not,
But spices spring in sweet array
From my pearl, precious, without spot.

Once, to that spot of which I rhyme,
I entered, in the arbour green,
In August, the high summer-time
When corn is cut with sickles keen;
Upon the mound where my pearl fell,
Tall, shadowing herbs grew bright and sheen,
Gilliflower, ginger and gromwell,
With peonies powdered all between.
As it was lovely to be seen,
So sweet the fragrance there, I wot,
Worthy her dwelling who hath been
My own pearl, precious, without spot.

Upon that spot my hands I crossed
In prayer, for cold at my heart caught,
And sudden sorrow surged and tossed,
Though reason reconcilement sought.
I mourned my pearl, dear beyond cost,
And strange fears with my fancy fought;
My will in wretchedness was lost,
And yet Christ comforted my thought.
Such odours to my sense were brought,
I fell upon that flowery plot,
Sleeping,--a sleep with dreams inwrought
Of my pearl, precious, without spot.

II

From the spot my spirit springs into space,
The while my body sleeping lies;

My ghost is gone in God's good grace,
Adventuring mid mysteries;
I know not what might be the place,
But I looked where tall cliffs cleave the skies,
Toward a forest I turned my face,
Where ranks of radiant rocks arise.
A man might scarce believe his eyes,
Such gleaming glory was from them sent;
No woven web may men devise
Of half such wondrous beauties blent.

In beauty shone each fair hillside
With crystal cliffs in shining row,
While bright woods everywhere abide,
Their boles as blue as indigo;
Like silver clear the leaves spread wide,
That on each spray thick-quivering grow;
If a flash of light across them glide
With shimmering sheen they gleam and glow;
The gravel on the ground below
Seemed precious pearls of Orient;
The sunbeams did but darkling show
So gloriously those beauties blent.

The beauty of the hills so fair
Made me forget my sufferings;
I breathed fruit fragrance fine and rare,
As if I fed on unseen things;
Brave birds fly through the woodland there,
Of flaming hues, and each one sings;
With their mad mirth may not compare
Cithern nor gayest citole-strings;
For when those bright birds beat their wings,
They sing together, all content;
Keen joy to any man it brings
To hear and see such beauties blent.

So beautiful was all the wood
Where, guided forth by Chance, I strayed,
There is no tongue that fully could
Describe it, though all men essayed.
Onward I walked in merriest mood
Nor any highest hill delayed
My feet. Far through the forest stood

The plain with fairest trees arrayed,
Hedges and slopes and rivers wide,
Like gold thread their banks' garnishment;
And when I won the waterside,
Dear Lord! what wondrous beauties blent!

The beauties of that stream were steep,
All-radiant banks of beryl bright;
Sweet-sighing did the water sweep,
With murmuring music running light;
Within its bed fair stones lay deep;
As if through glass they glowed, as white
As streaming stars when tired men sleep
Shine in the sky on a winter night.
Pure emerald even the pebbles seemed,
Sapphire, or other gems that lent
Luster, till all the water gleamed
With the glory of such beauties blent.

III

For the beauteousness of downs and dales,
Of wood and water and proud plains,
My joy springs up and my grief quails,
My anguish ends, and all my pains.
A swift stream down the valley hales
My feet along. Bliss brims my brains;
The farther I follow those watery vales,
The stronger joy my heart constrains.
While Fortune fares as her proud will deigns,
Sending solace or sending sore,
When a man her fickle favour gains,
He looketh to have aye more and more.

There was more of marvel and of grace
Than I could tell, howe'er I tried;
The human heart that could embrace
A tenth part were well satisfied;

For Paradise, the very place,
Must be upon that farther side;
The water by a narrow space
Pleasance from pleasance did divide.
Beyond, on some slope undescried
The City stood, I thought, wherefore
I strove to cross the river's tide,
And ever I longed, yet more and more.

More, and still more wistfully,
The banks beyond the brook I scanned;
If, where I stood, 't was fair to see,
Still lovelier lay that farther land.
I sought if any ford might be
Found, up or down, by rock or sand;
But perils plainer appeared to me,
The farther I strode along the strand;
I thought I ought not thus to stand
Timid, with such bright bliss before;
Then a new matter came to hand
That moved my heart yet more and more.

Marvels more and more amaze
My mind beyond that water fair:
From a cliff of crystal, splendid rays,
Reflected, quiver in the air.
At the cliff's foot a vision stays
My glance, a maiden debonaire,
All glimmering white before my gaze;
And I know her,--have seen her otherwhere.
Like fine gold leaf one cuts with care,
Shone the maiden on the farther shore.
Long time I looked upon her there,
And ever I knew her more and more.

As more and more I scanned her face
And form, when I had found her so,
A glory of gladness filled the place
Beyond all it was wont to show.
My joy would call her and give chase,
But wonder struck my courage low;
I saw her in so strange a place,
The shock turned my heart dull and slow.
But now she lifts that brow aglow,

Like ivory smooth, even as of yore,
It made my senses straying go,
It stung my heart aye more and more.

IV

More than I liked did my fear rise.
Stock still I stood and dared not call;
With lips close shut and watchful eyes,
I stood as quiet as hawk in hall.
I thought her a spirit from the skies;
I doubted what thing might befall;
If to escape me now she tries,
How shall my voice her flight forestall?
Then graciously and gay withal,
In royal robes, so sweet, so slight,
She rose, so modest and so small,
That precious one in pearls bedight.

Pearl bedight full royally,
Adown the bank with merry mien,
Came the maiden, fresh as fleur-de-lys.
Her surcoat linen must have been
Shining in whitest purity,
Slashed at the sides and caught between
With the fairest pearls, it seemed to me,
That ever yet mine eyes had seen;
With large folds falling loose, I ween,
Arrayed with double pearls, her white
Kirtle, of the same linen sheen,
With precious pearls all round was dight.

A crown with pearls bedight, the girl
Was wearing, and no other stone;
High pinnacled of clear white pearl,
Wrought as if pearls to flowers were grown.
No band nor fillet else did furl
The long locks all about her thrown.

Her air demure as duke or earl,
Her hue more white than walrus-bone;
Like sheer gold thread the bright hair strown
Loose on her shoulders, lying light.
Her colour took a deeper tone
With bordering pearls so fair bedight.

Bedight was every hem, and bound,
At wrists, sides, and each aperture,
With pearls the whitest ever found,--
White all her brave investiture;
But a wondrous pearl, a flawless round,
Upon her breast was set full sure;
A man's mind it might well astound,
And all his wits to madness lure.
I thought that no tongue might endure
Fully to tell of that sweet sight,
So was it perfect, clear and pure,
That precious pearl with pearls bedight.

Bedight in pearls, lest my joy cease,
That lovely one came down the shore;
The gladdest man from here to Greece,
The eagerest, was I, therefore;
She was nearer kin than aunt or niece,
And thus my joy was much the more.
She spoke to me for my soul's peace,
Courtesied with her quaint woman's lore,
Caught off the shining crown she wore,
And greeted me with glance alight.
I blessed my birth; my bliss brimmed o'er
To answer her in pearls bedight.

V

"O Pearl," I said, "in pearls bedight,
Art thou my pearl for which I mourn,
Lamenting all alone at night?

With hidden grief my heart is worn.
Since thou through grass didst slip from sight,
Pensive and pained, I pass forlorn,
And thou livest in a life of light,
A world where enters sin nor scorn.
What fate has hither my jewel borne,
And left me in earth's strife and stir?
Oh, sweet, since we in twain were torn,
I have been a joyless jeweler."

That Jewel then with gems besprent
Glanced up at me with eyes of grey,
Put on her pearl crown orient,
And soberly began to say:
"You tell your tale with wrong intent,
Thinking your pearl gone quite away.
Like a jewel within a coffer pent,
In this gracious garden bright and gay,
Your pearl may ever dwell at play,
Where sin nor mourning come to her;
It were a joy to thee alway
Wert thou a gentle jeweler.

"But, Jeweler, if thou dost lose
Thy joy for a gem once dear to thee,
Methinks thou dost thy mind abuse,
Bewildered by a fantasy;
Thou hast lost nothing save a rose
That flowered and failed by life's decree:
Because the coffer did round it close,
A precious pearl it came to be.
A thief thou hast dubbed thy destiny
That something for nothing gives thee, sir;
Thou blamest thy sorrow's remedy,
Thou art no grateful jeweler."

Like jewels did her story fall,
A jewel, every gentle clause;
"Truly," I said, "thou best of all!
My great distress thy voice withdraws.
I thought my pearl lost past recall,
My jewel shut within earth's jaws;
But now I shall keep festival,
And dwell with it in bright wood-shaws;

And love my Lord and all His laws,
Who hath brought this bliss. Ah! if I were
Beyond these waves, I should have cause
To be a joyful jeweler."

"Jeweler," said that Gem so dear,
"Why jest ye men, so mad ye be?
Three sayings thou hast spoken clear,
And unconsidered were all three;
Their meaning thou canst not come near,
Thy word before thy thought doth flee.
First, thou believest me truly here,
Because with eyes thou mayst me see;
Second, with me in this country
Thou wilt dwell, whatever may deter;
Third, that to cross here thou art free:
That may no joyful jeweler."

VI

The jeweler merits little praise,
Who loves but what he sees with eye,
And it were a discourteous phrase
To say our Lord would make a lie,
Who surely pledged thy soul to raise,
Though fate should cause thy flesh to die.
Thou dost twist His words in crooked ways
Believing only what is nigh;
This is but pride and bigotry,
That a good man may ill assume,
To hold no matter trustworthy
Till like a judge he hear and doom.

"Whate'er thy doom, dost thou complain
As man should speak to God most high?
Thou wouldst gladly dwell in this domain;
'T were best, methinks, for leave to apply.
Even so, perchance, thou pleadest in vain.

Across this water thou wouldst fly,--
To other end thou must attain.
Thy corpse to clay comes verily,--
In Paradise 't was ruined by
Our forefather. Now in the womb
Of dreary death each man must lie,
Ere God on this bank gives his doom."

"Doom me not, sweet, to my old fears
And pain again wherein I pine.
My pearl that, long, long lost, appears,
Shall I again forego, in fine?
Meet it, and miss it through more years?
Thou hast hurt me with that threat of thine.
For what serves treasure but for tears,
One must so soon his bliss resign?
I reck not how my days decline,
Though far from earth my soul seek room,
Parted from that dear pearl of mine.
Save endless dole what is man's doom?"

"No doom save pain and soul's distress?"
She answered: "Wherefore thinkst thou so?
For pain of parting with the less,
Man often lets the greater go.
'T were better thou thy fate shouldst bless,
And love thy God, through weal and woe;
For anger wins not happiness;
Who must, shall bear; bend thy pride low;
For though thou mayst dance to and fro,
Struggle and shriek, and fret and fume,
When thou canst stir not, swift nor slow,
At last, thou must endure His doom."

"Let God doom as He doth ordain;
He will not turn one foot aside;
Thy good deeds mount up but in vain,
Thou must in sorrow ever bide;
Stint of thy strife, cease to complain,
Seek His compassion safe and wide,
Thy prayer His pity may obtain,
Till Mercy all her might have tried.
Thy anguish He will heal and hide,
And lightly lift away thy gloom;

For, be thou sore or satisfied,
All is for Him to deal and doom."

VII

Doom me not, dearest damosel;
It is not for wrath nor bitterness,
If rash and raving thoughts I tell.
For sin my heart seethed in distress,
Like bubbling water in a well.
I cry God mercy, and confess.
Rebuke me not with words so fell;
I have lost all that my life did bless;
Comfort my sorrow and redress,
Piteously thinking upon this:
Grief and my soul thou hast made express
One music,--thou who wert my bliss.

"My bliss and bale, thou hast been both,
But joy by great grief was undone;
When thou didst vanish, by my troth,
I knew not where my Pearl was gone.
To lose thee now I were most loth.
Dear, when we parted we were one;
Now God forbid that we be wroth,
We meet beneath the moon or sun
So seldom. Gently thy words run,
But I am dust, my deeds amiss;
The mercy of Christ and Mary and John
Is root and ground of all my bliss."

"A blissful life I see thee lead,
The while that I am sorrow's mate;
Haply thou givest little heed
What might my burning hurt abate.
Since I may in thy presence plead,
I do beseech thee thou narrate,
Soberly, surely, word and deed,

What life is thine, early and late?
I am fain of thy most fair estate;
The high road of my joy is this,
That thou hast happiness so great;
It is the ground of all my bliss."

She said, "May bliss to thee betide,"
Her face with beauty beaming clear,
"Welcome thou art here to abide,
For now thy speech is to me dear.
Masterful mood and haughty pride,
I warn thee win but hatred here;
For my Lord loveth not to chide
And meek are all that to Him come near.
When in His place thou shalt appear,
To kneel devout be not remiss,
My Lord the Lamb loveth such cheer,
Who is the ground of all my bliss."

"Thou sayest a blissful life I know,
And thou wouldst learn of its degree.
Thou rememberest when thy pearl fell low
In earth, I was but young to see;
But my Lord the Lamb, as if to show
His grace, took me His bride to be,
Crowned me a queen in bliss to go
Through length of days eternally;
And dowered with all His wealth is she
Who is His love, and I am His;
His worthiness and royalty
Are root and ground of all my bliss."

VIII

"My blissful one, may this be true.
Pardon if I speak ill," I prayed:
"Art thou the queen o' the heaven's blue,
To whom earth's honour shall be paid?

We believe in Mary, of grace who grew,
A mother, yet a blameless maid;
To wear her crown were only due
To one who purer worth displayed.
For perfectness by none gainsaid,
We call her the Phoenix of Araby,
That flies in faultless charm arrayed,
Like to the Queen of courtesy."

"Courteous Queen," that bright one said,
And, kneeling, lifted up her face:
"Matchless Mother and merriest Maid,
Blessèd Beginner of every grace."
Then she arose, and softly stayed,
And spoke to me across that space:
"Sir, many seek gain here, and are paid,
But defrauders are none within this place;
That Empress may all heaven embrace,
And earth and hell in her empery;
Her from her heritage none will chase,
For she is Queen of courtesy."

"The court of the kingdom of God doth thrive
Only because of this wondrous thing:
Each one who therein may arrive,
Of the realm is either queen or king;
And no one the other doth deprive,
But is fain of his fellow's guerdoning,
And would wish each crown might be worth five,
If possible were their bettering.
But my Lady, from whom our Lord did spring,
Rules over all our company,
And for that we all rejoice and sing,
Since she is Queen of courtesy."

"Of courtesy, as says St. Paul,
Members of Christ we may be seen.
As head and arm and leg, and all,
Bound to the body close have been,
Each Christian soul himself may call
A living limb of his Lord, I ween.
And see how neither hate nor gall
'Twixt limb and limb may intervene;
The head shows neither spite nor spleen,

Though arm and finger jewelled be,
So fare we all in love serene,
As kings and queens by courtesy."

"Courtesy flowers thy folk among,
And charity, I well believe.
If foolish words flow from my tongue,
Let not my speech thy spirit grieve.
A queen in heaven while yet so young,
Too high thou dost thyself upheave.
Then what reward from strife were wrung?
What worship more might he achieve
Who lived in penance morn and eve,
Through bodily pain in bliss to be?
Honour more high might he receive,
Than be crowned king by courtesy?"

IX

"That courtesy rewards no deed
If all be true that thou dost say;
Our life not two years didst thou lead
Nor learned to please God, nor to pray,
No Paternoster knew nor creed,
And made a queen on the first day!
I may not think, so God me speed!
That God from right would swerve away;
As a countess, damsel, by my fay!
To live in heaven were a fair boon,
Or like a lady of less array,
But a queen! Ah, no! it is too soon."

"With Him there is no soon nor late,"
Replied to me that worthy wight;
"True always is His high mandate;
He doth no evil, day nor night.
Hear Matthew in the mass narrate,
In the Gospel of the God of might,

His parable portrays the state
Of the Kingdom of Heaven, clear as light:
'My servants,' saith He, 'I requite
As a lord who will his vineyard prune;
The season of the year is right,
And labourers must be hired soon.'"

"Right soon the hirelings all may see
How the master with the dawn arose;
To hire his labourers forth went he,
And workmen stout and strong he chose.
For a penny a day they all agree,
Even as the master doth propose,
They toil and travail lustily,
Prune, bind, and with a ditch enclose.
Then to the market-place he goes,
And finds men idle at high noon:
'How can a man stand here who knows
The vineyards should be tilled so soon?'"

"'Soon as day dawned we hither won,
And no man hath our labour sought;
We have been standing since rose the sun
And no one bids us to do aught.'
'Enter my vineyard every one,'
The master answered quick as thought:
'The work that each by night has done
I will truly pay, withholding naught.'
Among the vines they went and wrought,
While morning, noon and afternoon,
More labourers the master brought,
Until the night must gather soon."

"Soon fell the time of evensong.
An hour before the sun was set,
He saw more idlers, young and strong;
His voice was sober with regret:
'Why stand ye idle all day long?'
'No man,' they said, 'hath hired us yet.'
'Go to my vineyard, fear no wrong;
Each man an honest wage shall get.'
The day grew dark and darker yet,
"Before the rising of the moon;
The master who would pay his debt,

Bade summon all the hirelings soon."

X

"The lord soon called his steward: 'Go
Bring in the men quick as ye may;
Give them the wages that I owe,
And, lest they aught against me say,
Range them along here in a row,
To each alike his penny pay;
Start with the last who standeth low,
And to the first proceed straightway,'
And then the first began to pray,
Complaining they had travailed sore:
'These wrought but one hour of the day,
We think we should receive the more.'"

"'More have we served,' they muttered low,
'Who have endured the long day's heat,
Than these who not two hours toiled so;
Why should their claim with ours compete?'
Said the master: 'I pay all I owe;
Friend, no injustice shalt thou meet;
Take that which is thine own and go.
For a penny we settled in the street;
Why dost thou now for more entreat?
Thou wast well satisfied before.
Once made, a bargain is complete;
Why shouldst thou, threatening, ask for more?"

"'What can be more within my gift
Than what I will with mine to do?
Let not thine eyes to evil shift,
Because I trusty am, and true.'
'Thus I,' said Christ, 'all men shall sift.
The last shall be the first of you;
And the first last, however swift,
For many are called, but chosen, few.'

And thus poor men may have their due,
That late and little burden bore;
Their work may vanish like the dew,
The mercy of God is much the more."

"More gladness have I, herewithin,
Of flower of life, and noble name,
Than all men in the world might win,
Who thought their righteous deeds to name.
Nathless even now did I begin;
To the vineyard as night fell I came,
But my Lord would not account it sin;
He paid my wages without blame.
Yet others did not fare the same,
Who toiled and travailed there before,
And of their hire might nothing claim,
Perchance shall not for a year more."

Then more, and openly, I spake:
"From thy tale no reason can I wring;
God's righteousness doth ever wake,
Else Holy Writ is a fabled thing.
From the Psalter one verse let us take,
That may to a point this teaching bring:
'Thou requitest each for his deed's sake,
Thou high and all-foreknowing King.'
If one man to his work did cling
All day, and thou wert paid before,
Most wage falls to least labouring,
And ever the less receives the more."

XI

"Of more or less where God doth reign,
There is no chance," she gently said,
"For, whether large or small his gain,
Here every man alike is paid.
No niggard churl our High Chieftain,

But lavishly His gifts are made,
Like streams from a moat that flow amain,
Or rushing waves that rise unstayed.
Free were his pardon whoever prayed
Him who to save man's soul did vow,
Unstinted his bliss, and undelayed,
For the grace of God is great enow."

"But now thou wouldst my wit checkmate,
Making my wage as wrong appear;
Thou say'st that I am come too late,
Of so large hire to be worthy here;
Yet sawest thou ever small or great,
Living in prayer and holy fear,
Who did not forfeit at some date
The meed of heaven to merit clear?
Nay much the rather, year by year,
All bend from right and to evil bow;
Mercy and grace their way must steer,
For the grace of God is great enow."

"But enow of grace have the innocent
New-born, before the sacred shrine,
They are sealed with water in sacrament,
And thus are brought into the vine.
Anon the day with darkness blent,
Death by its might makes to decline;
Who wrought no wrong ere hence they went,
The gentle Lord receives, in fine;
They obeyed His will, they bore His sign,
Why should He not their claim allow?
Yea, and reward them, I opine,
For the grace of God is great enow."

"'T is known enow that all mankind
At first were formed for perfect bliss;
Our forefather that boon resigned,
All for an apple's sake, I wis;
We fell condemned, for folly blind,
To suffer sore in hell's abyss;
But One a remedy did find
Lest we our hope of heaven should miss.
He suffered on the cross for this,
Red blood ran from His crownèd brow;

He saved us by that pain of His,
For the grace of God is great enow."

"Enow there flowed from out that well,
Blood and water from His broad wound:
The blood bought us from bale of hell,
And from second death deliverance found.
The water is baptism, truth to tell,
That followed-the spear so sharply ground,
And washes away the guilt most fell
Of those that Adam in death had drowned.
Now is there nothing in earth's great round,
To bar from the bliss wherewith God did endow
Mankind,--restored to us safe and sound,
For the grace of God is great enow."

XII

"Grace enow a man may get
By penitence, though he sin again;
But with long sorrow and regret,
He must bear punishment and pain;
But righteous reason will not let
The innocent be hurt in vain;
God never gave His judgment yet,
That they should suffer who show no stain.
The sinful soul of mercy fain
Finds pardon if he will repent,
But he who sinless doth remain
Is surely saved, being innocent."

"Two men are saved of God's good grace,
Who severally have done His will:
The righteous man shall see His face,
The innocent dwells with Him still.
In the Psalter thou may'st find a case:
'Lord, who shall climb to Thy high hill,
Or rest within Thy Holy Place?'

The psalmist doth the sense fulfill:
'Who with his hands did never ill,
His heart to evil never lent,
There to ascend he shall have skill;'
So surely saved is the innocent."

"That the righteous is saved I hold certain;
Before God's palace he shall stand
Who never took man's life in vain,
Who never to flatter his fellow planned.
Of the righteous, the Wise Man writeth plain
How kindly our King doth him command;
In ways full strait he doth restrain,
Yet shows him the kingdom great and grand,
As who saith: 'Behold! yon lovely land!
Thou may'st win it, if so thy will be bent.'
But with never peril on either hand,
Surely saved is the innocent."

"Of the righteous saved, hear one man say--
David, who in the Psalter cried:
'O Lord, call never Thy servant to pay,
For no man living is justified.'
So thou, if thou shalt come one day
To the court that each cause must decide,
For mercy with justice thou may'st pray
Through this same text that I espied.
But may He on the bloody cross that died,
His holy hands with hard nails rent,
Give thee to pass when thou art tried,
Saved, not as righteous, but innocent."

"Of the sinless saved the tale is told,--
Read in the Book where it is said:
When Jesus walked, among men of old,
The people a passage to Him made;
Bringing their bairns for Him to hold,
For the blessing of His hand they prayed.
The twelve reproved them: 'Overbold
To seek the Master;' and sternly stayed.
But Jesus said: 'Be ye not afraid;
Suffer the children, nor prevent;
God's kingdom is for such arrayed.'
Surely saved are the innocent."

XIII

"Christ called to Him the innocents mild,
And said His kingdom no man might win,
Unless he came thither as a child,--Not
otherwise might he enter in,
Harmless, faithful, undefiled,
With never a spot of soiling sin,--For
these whom the world has not beguiled
Gladly shall one the gate unpin.
There shall that endless bliss begin,
The merchant sought, and straight was led
To barter all stuffs men weave and spin,
To buy him a pearl unblemished."

"'This pearl unblemished, bought so dear,
For which the merchant his riches gave,
Is like the kingdom of heaven clear;'
So said the Father of world and wave.
It is a flawless, perfect sphere,
Polished and pure, and bright and brave;
As on my heart it doth appear,
It is common to all who to virtue clave.
My Lord, the Lamb Who died to save,
Here set it in token of His blood shed
For peace. Then let the wild world rave,
But buy thee this pearl unblemishèd."

"O Pearl unblemished, in pure pearls dressed,
That beareth," said I, "the pearl of price,
Who formed thy figure-and thy vest?
Truly he wrought with cunning nice;
For thy beauty, above nature's best,
Passeth Pygmalion's artifice;
Nor Aristotle the lore possessed
To depict in words so fair device.
Than fleur-de-lys thou art fairer thrice,

Angel-mannered and courtly bred,--
Tell to me truly: in Paradise
What meaneth the pearl unblemished?"

"My spotless Lamb, who all doth heal,"
She answered, "my dear Destiny,
Chose me in marriage bond to seal;
Unfit, He graced me regally,
From your world's woe come into weal.
He called me of His courtesy:
'Come hither to me, my lover leal,
For mote nor spot is none in thee.'
He gave me my might and great beauty;
He washed my weeds in His blood so red,
And crowned me, forever clean to be,
And clothed me in pearls unblemishèd."

"Unblemished bride, bright to behold,
That royalty hath so rich and rare,
What is this Lamb, that thou hast told
How for wedded wife He called thee there?
Above all others dost thou make bold,
As His chosen lady His life to share?
So many, comely in combs of gold,
For Christ have lived in strife and care,
Must these to a lower place repair,
That never any with Him may wed,
Save only thyself, so proud and fair,
Peerless Queen, and unblemished?"

XIV

"Unblemished," answered she again,
"Without a spot of black or gray,
With honour may I this maintain;
But 'peerless Queen' I did not say.
Brides of the Lamb in bliss we reign,
An hundred and forty thousand gay,

As in the Apocalypse is made plain,
Saint John beheld them on a day;
On the hill of Zion he saw them stay,
In vision his spirit looked on them,
For the wedding clad in bright-array,
At the city of New Jerusalem."

"Of Jerusalem in speech I tell;
And what He is if thou wouldst see--
My Lamb, my Lord, my dear Jewel,
My Joy, my Love, my Bliss so free,--
The prophet Isaiah writeth well
Of His most mild humility:
'Guiltless, when men upon Him fell
For never a fault nor felony,
As a sheep to the slaughter led was He;
Quiet, the while the crowd contemn,
As a lamb in the shearer's hands might be,
He was judged by Jews in Jerusalem.'"

"In Jerusalem was my Lover slain,
Rent on the rood by ruffians bold;
To bear our ills He was full fain,
To suffer our sorrows manifold;
Buffeted until blood did stain
That face so lovely to behold;
He took upon Him all sin and pain,
Even He of Whom not one sin is told;
On the rude cross stretched faint and cold,
He let men deride him and condemn;
Meek as a lamb, betrayed and sold,
He died for us in Jerusalem."

"At Jerusalem, Jordan and Galilee,
Wherever Saint John came to baptize,
His words with Isaiah's words agree.
On Jesus he lifted up his eyes,
Speaking of Him this prophecy:
'Behold the Lamb of God!' he cries:
'Who bears the world's sins, this is He!
The guilt of all upon Him lies,
Though He wrought evil in no wise.
The branches springing from that stem
Who can recount? 'T is He who dies

For our sake in Jerusalem.'"

"In Jerusalem my Lover sweet
Twice as a lamb did thus appear,
Even as the prophets both repeat,
So meek the mien that He did wear;
The third time also, as is meet,
In the Revelation is written clear.
Reading a book on His high seat
Midmost the throne that saints ensphere,
The Apostle John beheld Him near;
That book seven sacred seals begem;
And at that sight all folk felt fear
In hell, in earth and Jerusalem."

XV

This Jerusalem Lamb had never stain
Of other hue than perfect white,
That showeth neither streak nor strain
Of soil, but is like wool to sight;
And souls that free of sin remain
The Lamb receiveth with delight;
And, though each day a group we gain,
There comes no strife for room nor right,
Nor rivalry our bliss to blight.
The more the merrier, I profess.
In company our love grows bright,
In honour more and never less.

"Lessening of bliss no comer brings
To us who bear this pearl at breast;
Nor show they flaws nor tarnishings
Who wear such pure pearls like a crest.
Though round our corpses the clay clings,
And though ye mourn us without rest,
Knowledge have we of goodly things.
Through the first death our hope we test;

Grief goes; at each mass we are blest
By the Lamb Who gives us happiness;
The bliss of each is bright and best,
And no one's honour is the less."

"That thou my tale the less may doubt,
In the Revelation 'tis told, and more:
'I saw,' says John, 'a goodly rout
The hill of Zion covering o'er,
The Lamb, with maidens round about,
An hundred thousand and forty and four,
And each brow, fairly written out,
The Lamb's name and His Father's bore.
Then a sound from heaven I heard outpour,
As streams, full laden, foam and press,
Or as thunders among dark crags roar,
The tumult was, and nothing less."

"'Nathless, though high that shout might ring,
And loud the voices sounding near,
A strain full new I heard them sing,
And sweet and strange it was to hear.
Like harper's hands upon the string
Was that new song they sang so clear;
The noble notes went vibrating,
And gentle words came to my ear.
Close by God's throne, without one fear,
Where the four beasts His power confess,
And the elders stand so grave of cheer,
They sang their new song, none the less."

"'Nathless is none with skill so fine,
For all the crafts that ever he knew,
That of that song might sing a line;
Save these that hold the Lamb in view;
From earth brought to that land divine,
As first fruits that to God are due,
They serve the Lamb and bear His sign,
As like Himself in face and hue;
For never lying nor tale untrue
Defiled their lips in life's distress;'
Whatever might move them, they but drew
Nearer the Master, none the less."

"Nevertheless, speak out I must,
My Pearl, though queries rude I pose.
To try thy fair wit were unjust
Whom Christ to His own chamber chose.
Behold, I am but dung and dust,
And thou a rare and radiant rose,
Abiding here in life, and lust
Of loveliness that ever grows.
A hind that no least cunning knows,
I needs must my one doubt express;
Though boisterous as the wind that blows,
Let my prayer move thee none the less."

XVI

Yet, none the less, on thee I call,
If thou wilt listen verily,
As thou art glorious over all,
Hearken the while I question thee.
Within some splendid castle wall,
Have ye not dwellings fair to see?
Of David's city, rich, royal,
Jerusalem, thou tellest me.
In Palestine its place must be;
In wildwood such none ever saw.
Since spotless is your purity,
Your dwellings should be free from flaw.

"Now this most fair and flawless rout,
Thronging thousands, as thou dost tell,
They must possess, beyond a doubt,
A sightly city wherein to dwell.
'T were strange that they should live without;
For so bright a band it were not well;
Yet I see no building hereabout.
Dost thou linger as in a woodland cell,
Alone and hidden, for the spell
Of rushing stream and shining shaw?

If thou hast a dwelling beyond this dell,
Now show me that city free from flaw."

"Not flawless the city in Juda's land,"
That gentle one gently to me spake,
"But the Lamb did bless it when He planned
To suffer there sorely for man's sake.
That is the old city we understand,
And there the bonds of old guilt did break;
But the new, alighted from God's hand,
The Apostle John for his theme did take.
The Lamb Who is white with never a flake
Of black, did thither His fair folk draw;
For His flock no fenced fold need He make,
Nor moat for His city free from flaw."

"To figure flawlessly what may mean
Jerusalems twain: the first of those
Was 'the Sight of Peace' as it is seen
In the word of God, for the gospel shows
How there our peace made sure hath been,
Since to suffer therein the Saviour chose;
In the other is always peace to glean,
Peace that never an ending knows.
To that city bright the spirit goes
When the flesh hath fallen beneath death's law;
There glorious gladness forever grows
For His fair folk that are free from flaw."

"Flawless maid so mild and meek,"
Then said I to that lovely flower:
"Let me that stately city seek,
And let me see thy blissful bower."
That bright one said, "Thou art too weak,
Thou may'st not enter to its tower;
Yet of the Lamb I did bespeak
This goodly gift, that He would dower
Thine eyes with the sight for one short hour,--
From without,--within none ever saw;
To step in that street thou hast no power,
Unless thy soul were free from flaw."

XVII

"This flawless sight I will not hide;
Up toward the brook's head thou must go,
While I will follow on this side,
Till yonder hill the city show."
And then I would no longer bide,
But stole through branches, bending low,
Till from the summit I espied,
Through green boughs swaying to and fro,
Afar, the city, all aglow,
That brighter than bright sunbeams shone.
In writing it is pictured so,
In the Revelation of St. John.

As John the Apostle saw the sight,
I saw that city, standing near
Jerusalem, so royal dight,
As if from Heaven alighted here.
The city all of gold burned bright,
Like gleaming glass that glistens clear.
With precious stones beneath set right:
Foundations twelve of gems most dear,
Wrought wondrous richly, tier on tier.
Each base was of a separate stone
As, perfectly, it doth appear
In the Revelation of St. John.

John named the stones that he had seen,
I knew the order that he made;
The first a jasper must have been,
That on the lowest base was laid,
Beneath the rest it glinted green;
A sapphire in the second grade;
Chalcedony, from blemish clean,
In the third course was fair arrayed;
Fourth, emerald, of greenest shade,
Fifth, sardonyx, was raised thereon;
The sixth a ruby, as is said
In the Revelation of St. John.

John joined to these the chrysolite,
The seventh gem in that basement;
The eighth, a beryl, clear and white;
The topaz, ninth, its luster lent;
Tenth, chrysophrase, both soft and bright;
Eleventh, the jacinth, translucent;
And twelfth, and noblest to recite,
Amethyst, blue with purple blent.
The wall above those basements went
Jasper, like glass that glistening shone;
I saw, as the story doth present,--
The Revelation of St. John.

I saw, as John doth clear devise:
The great stones rose like a broad stair;
Above, the city, to my eyes,
In height, length, breadth appeared four-square;
The jasper wall shone amber-wise,
The golden streets as glass gleamed fair;
The dwellings glowed in glorious guise
With every stone most rich and rare.
Each length of bright wall builded there
For full twelve furlongs' space stretched on,
And height, length, breadth all equal were:
"I saw one mete it," writeth John.

XVIII

As John doth write more met mine eye:
Within each wall were set three gates;
Twelve in succession I could spy,
Portals adorned with bright gold plates;
Each gate a single pearl saw I,
A perfect pearl, as John relates.
On each a name was written high
Of Israel's sons after their dates,
The oldest first, as the story states.

Within those streets by night or noon,
Light beams that not one hour abates;
They needed neither sun nor moon.

Of sun or moon they had no need;
For God Himself was their lamp light,
The Lamb their lantern was indeed;
From Him the city shone all bright.
Through wall and dwelling my looks might speed,
Such clearness could not hinder sight.
Of the high throne ye might take heed,
With draperies of radiant white,
As John the Apostle doth endite;
High God Himself did sit thereon.
From the throne a river welled outright
Was brighter than both sun and moon.

Sun nor moon shone never so sweet
As the full flood of that bright stream;
Swiftly it swept through every street,
Untainted did the water gleam.
Chapel nor church mine eyes did meet;
Therein is no temple as I deem;
The Almighty is their minster meet,
The Lamb their sacrifice supreme.
The gates with neither bolt nor beam,
Wide open stand at night and noon;
To enter there let no man dream
Whom sin hath stained beneath the moon.

The moon may there win no least might,
She is too spotty, grey and grim;
Therein, moreover, is never night,
Why should the moon fill full her rim
To rival the all-glorious light
That beams upon the river's brim?
The planets are in poorest plight;
The sun itself is far too dim.
Beside the stream trees tall and trim
Bear living fruits that none doth prune;
Twelve times a year bends low each limb,
Renewed with fruitage every moon.

Beneath the moon full well might fail
The heart of mortal to endure
The marvel that did mine eyes assail,
Fashioned the fancy to allure.
I stood as still as a startled quail,
For wonder of its fair figure,
I felt no rest and no travail,
Ravished before such radiance pure.
I say, and with conviction sure,
Had the eyes of man received that boon,
Though wisest clerks sought for his cure,
His life were lost beneath the moon.

XIX

Now, even as the full moon might rise
Ere daylight doth to darkness fall,
Sudden I saw with still surprise
Within that shining city-wall,
The streets full-thronged in wondrous wise,
Silent, with never a herald's call,
With virgins in the selfsame guise
As my beloved, sweet and small.
Each head was crowned with coronal,
Pearl-wrought, and every robe was white;
On each breast bound, imperial,
The Pearl of Price with great delight.

With great delight together going
On glassy golden streets they tread;
To a hundred thousand swiftly growing,
And all alike were they garmented:
The gladdest face who could be knowing?
The Lamb did proudly pass ahead,
His seven horns of clear red gold glowing,
His robes like pearls high valuèd.
On toward the throne their way they thread,
None crowded in that band so bright,
But mild as maidens when mass is said,

So fared they forth with great delight.

The great delight His coming gave,
It were too much for me to tell.
When He approached the Elders grave,
Prone there before His feet they fell;
Legions of summoned angels brave
Swayed censers of the sweetest smell;
With music like a mighty wave,
All sang in praise of that gay Jewel.
The hymn might strike through earth to hell
That with joy those hosts of heaven recite;
To praise the Lamb I liked full well,
Amid the group in great delight.

Delighted, I would fain devise
His loveliness, with mind intent:
First was He, blithest, best to prize,
Of all on whom man's speech is spent;
So nobly white His draperies,
Such grace His simple glances lent;
But a wide, wet wound my gaze descries
Beneath His heart, through His skin rent;
Down His white side the blood was sent.
Alas! I thought, what scorn or spite
Could any human heart have bent
In such a deed to take delight?

The Lamb's delight might no man doubt,
Though that wide wound His hurt displayed,
From His fair face looked lovely out
Glad glances, glorious, unafraid,
I looked upon His shining rout,
With fullest life so bright arrayed,
My little queen there moved about,
I had thought beside me in the glade.
Ah Lord! how much of mirth she made!
Among her peers she was so white!
The stream I surely needs must wade,
For longing love, in great delight.

XX

Delight that flooded eye and ear
My mortal mind beatified;
When I saw her, I must reach my dear,
Though she beyond the brook abide.
Nothing, I thought, could keep me here,
No crippling blow hold my strength tied;
I would plunge, whatever interfere,
And swim the stream, though there I died.
But ere the water I had tried,
Even as I would my vow fulfill,
From my purpose I was turned aside;
It was not to my Prince's will.

My wilful purpose pleased not Him,
That I with headlong zeal essayed;
Though I was rash of thought and limb,
Yet suddenly my deed was stayed.
As I sprang forward to the brim,
The action in my dreaming made
Me waken in my arbour trim.
My head upon the mound was laid
Where my pearl to the grass once strayed.
I stretched my body, frightened, chill,
And, sighing, to myself I said:
"Now all be to the Prince's will."

Against my will was I exiled
From that bright region, fair and fain,
From that life, glad and undefiled,
And longing dulled my sense again;
I swooned in sorrow for the child,
Needs must my heart cry and complain:
"O Pearl, dear was thy counsel mild,
In this true vision of my brain!
If very truth divide us twain;
If thou goest crowned, secure from ill,
Well for me in my prison-pain
That thou art to the Prince's will."

To the Prince's will had my heart bent,
And sought but what to me was given,
Held fast to that, with true intent,
As my Pearl prayed me out of heaven;
Did I to God my thoughts present,
More in His mysteries had I thriven.
But a man will seek more than is sent,
Till from his hand his hope be riven.
Thus from my joy was I forth driven,
From the life upon that holy hill.
Oh, fools, that with the Lord have striven,
Or proffered gifts against his will!

The Prince's will to serve aright
The Christian may full well divine;
For I have found Him, day and night,
A God, a Lord, a Friend in fine.
Upon this mound my soul hath sight,
Where I for piteous sorrow pine;
My Pearl to God I pledge and plight,
With Christ's dear blessing and with mine,--
His, who, in form of bread and wine,
The priest doth daily show us still.
His servants may we be, or shine,
Pure pearls, according to his will.

THE END